ONE FOR ME, ONE FOR YOU

In this book you will find four lively read-aloud stories about Melanie and her younger sister Flora, who live in the Caribbean and are always getting into trouble!

Rita Phillips Mitchell was born in Belize, Central America. She trained as a teacher in Kingston, Jamaica, before moving to Britain where she taught in primary schools for many years. She currently works part-time as a teacher and counsellor to refugees. She is the author of *Hue Boy* (illustrated by Caroline Binch), which won the 0-5 category of the 1993 Smarties Book Prize. She lives in London.

Paul Howard graduated from Leicester Polytechnic in 1989 with a Graphics BA. He has illustrated a number of stories for Walker, including *Friends Next Door*, *A Very Special Birthday*, *Taking the Cat's Way Home*, *Jim's Winter* and the picture books *John Joe and the Big Hen*, *Rosie's Fishing Trip* and *A Year in the City*.

ONE FOR ME, ONE FOR YOU

Written by
RITA PHILLIPS MITCHELL

Illustrated by
PAUL HOWARD

WALKER BOOKS
AND SUBSIDIARIES
LONDON · BOSTON · SYDNEY

For Leanne and Saphire
and for all other sisters
who have got little Floras
RPM

For Adele and Alexander
PH

First published 1995 by Walker Books Ltd
87 Vauxhall Walk, London SE11 5HJ

2 4 6 8 10 9 7 5 3

Text © 1995 Rita Phillips Mitchell
Illustrations © 1995 Paul Howard

The right of Rita Phillips Mitchell to be identified as author of this
book has been asserted by her in accordance with the Copyright,
Design and Patents Act 1988.

This book has been typeset in Plantin Light.

Printed in England

British Library Cataloguing in Publication Data
A catalogue record for this book is available from the
British Library.

ISBN 0-7445-2483-0 (hb)
ISBN 0-7445-4381-9 (pb)

CONTENTS

"I'm bored," moaned Flora, "and I hate standing under this boring mango tree."

One for Me, One for You

It was Saturday. My mother had gone to the market. My father was getting ready to go out and singing at the top of his voice. Flora – my little sister – and me were in the back garden standing in the shade of the big mango tree. This was what we did when we were very hot and fed up and couldn't think of anything interesting to do.

"I'm bored," moaned Flora. "I'm bored and I hate standing under this boring mango tree."

"Trees aren't boring," I said.

"Well, it's supposed to grow mangoes and any tree that doesn't do what it's supposed to is dead boring," said Flora.

"It's too old, I guess," I said.

"Old. What do you mean? It looks OK to me," said Flora.

"People grow old, trees grow old. Great Grandma told me that this tree has been through great storms and a fire, and it was long time old even when she was a girl."

"You're kidding, Melanie! You mean to say that this mango tree is older than Great Grandma?" said Flora, raising her voice. "Then this tree isn't just old, it's older than very old. No wonder it hasn't grown any proper eating mangoes in a long while."

We stood there, lost in thought, till a racket above our heads cut into the silence. The noises were the kind birds make when they are excited. I was sweating buckets – even standing still was too much like hard work – and I couldn't be bothered to look up. But of course Flora had to investigate. She stood back, swivelled her head and scanned each branch like she was a searchlight.

And very soon she started to jump up and down like a mad thing, her long black plaits bobbing about on her shoulders. She wasn't bored any more.

"Look, Mel, look!" She pointed to two mangoes at the top of the tree.

We couldn't believe our eyes. They were bottle green and glistening. Large leaves of a darker green formed an umbrella over them.

"What a super hiding place," said Flora. "The greedy birds won't be able to see them."

"Maybe they have already," I said.

"In any case they're too green and hard for their beaks," said Flora.

"That's a bit of luck for us then," I said.

"Us?" said Flora. "I saw them first."

I ignored her. "We must guard them. They're our little secret. Right?"

"Right," Flora said. "But they're two secrets really, and from now on let's call them... One for me and one for you. That way nobody will guess what we're talking about. Get it?"

"Get it," I said.

Then together we repeated, "One for me and one for you."

From then on we watched that mango tree like hawks. We shooshed the birds away and watched for caterpillars. During the dry season we did a rain dance and when that didn't work we doused the roots of the tree with buckets of water. At nights we took turns to guard it from our window. Whenever one of us was caught sleeping on the job, the other one would scold, "Some

During the dry season we did a rain dance.

watchman you'd make!"

The days went by. Both of us were impatient for the mangoes to grow and ripen, but Flora got so bad, her imagination sometimes played tricks on her and she would say, "I'm sure I can hear one for me and one for you growing."

We guarded our secrets well and our secrets did grow and they kept right on growing until they were big and beautiful and ready for picking.

"I like the one that's half green and half red," I said.

"OK by me," said Flora. "Because I want the one that's the colour of the sun."

"Wanting and getting are two different things," I said. "You can't just stand there. You've got to do something like hitting, shaking or something else."

Flora plumped for something else. Spreading her skirt open wide she stood under the two mangoes and chanted, "Mango, mango, up so high. I must eat you before I die. Twirl round, fall down. Do it now. My skirt is wide, just plop inside."

"Only a real dumbhead would talk to mangoes," I said, picking up a stick.

I tried to hit the mangoes down but the stick only touched the lower branches each time. Then I began to throw anything I could get my hands on.

"You can't reach," said Flora.

"Any brilliant ideas then, smarty pants?" I asked.

"Yep."

"What?"

"Not telling," said Flora, looking at me wide-eyed. Then she started to grin. Mischief was written all over her face.

"You thinking something you shouldn't be thinking, Flora?"

"Maybe, and again maybe not."

"You thinking what I'm thinking, then?"

"Don't know."

"I bet you are."

"Well, I bet you can't and you won't because you're a scaredy cat."

I hated to admit it but Flora was real clever. She knew I could never resist a dare.

"You just watch," I said, walking towards the trunk of the tree. Flora watched from a safe distance, half warning, half egging me on.

"Go on then … the branches will break and you'll fall down … like rock-a-bye baby in the treetop."

Our mother had told us never to climb the mango tree. If she caught me I would be in big trouble, but she was at the market and I reckoned I was safe.

I wedged one foot in the fork of the first branch and the other on a second branch just above. After that it was easy-peasy climbing up.

My mango was the nearest, so I picked it first. "One for me," I said, and put it in my pocket. Then I picked Flora's. It was golden and glistening, like a small warm sun in my hand. I parted the branches and shouted down, "Spread open your skirt. Quick. Catch. One for you is coming."

Flora quickly opened her skirt, making a well in the middle. And the mango dropped in with a great PLOP.

She caught hold of it and set to work with her teeth right away. Flora created such a din eating that mango – munching, slurping, licking her fingers and smacking her lips – my great-grandmother would've said it was

"This is nectar fit for the gods," I said to myself.

enough to wake the dead.

"Momma will be a long time at the market," I told myself. "No need to hurry down." And I started eating too, and the sweet juice flowed down my throat.

"This is nectar fit for the gods," I said to myself – another saying of my great-grandmother's. She always said it when she drank her home-made cashew wine.

After a while, Flora's munching, slurping and licking noises stopped and things went quiet down below. I should've taken notice, but I didn't. I was far too busy trying to suck my mango right down to the dry seed. I took a lick... "Dry as a bone," I thought. I took another lick and another... "Dry as a stone. When I'm finished with this mango seed, not even a bird without ambition will want it."

"Me-la-nieeeeee!" My mother's voice

came zooming through the air.

It sounded like a roll of thunder. It sounded like fire engines. It sounded like a hundred police sirens. I looked down through the leaves. My mother stood tall with her hands on her hips. She looked fierce. Her eyes flashed fire. The mango tree trembled and I trembled with it. A branch cracked below my feet.

"Melanie, come down from that tree this instant," said my mother.

The ground seemed a long way away. "I can't get down," I said in a small voice.

"You can and you will," said my mother in a big voice.

"What's all the racket about?" asked my father, coming towards us.

"I'm scared the branch is going to break," I cried. My father would find a way to get me out of the mango tree but I didn't know how. I held my breath and hoped and waited.

I watched as my father walked away and disappeared into the shed. Meanwhile my mother folded her arms and stared up at me. Flora had a look on her face that said, "I'm glad it's not me and, oh boy, you're in a lot of trouble."

I felt silly. Then suddenly I felt angry. I stopped being afraid and found my feet again. I climbed down a few branches and then jumped. I landed on the soft mound of leaves and grass, just as my father came back with a ladder.

I was tempted to say, "Thanks very much but no thanks." But I was in enough trouble already.

My father leaned the ladder against a wall. Then he threw back his head and spread out his arms. Like he wanted to be a tree himself.

"You know how very oooooold your great-gran is, Melanie?" he asked.

I nodded.

"This tree is older than her. If you ask me, it's suffering from aches and creaks just like your great-gran. What do you suppose would happen if you climbed all over your very oooold great-gran?"

I nearly laughed out loud, but my mother was watching me.

"You want to break your neck?" she said. "To hit your head and get fool-fool? Next time you so much as go near that tree I shall teach you the lesson of your life. I'll let you stay up there."

I knew that my mother didn't mean it – she just wanted to scare me. She paused, then said, "Look at your little sister! She's filthy and it's all down to you."

Flora cried right on cue.

"Look what you've done," said my mother. She hugged Flora. "There, there, my little flower." Flora bawled all the louder. I glowered at her. Looking at her bawling face, I tried hard to imagine what kind of flower my mother meant. And then it came in a flash when I noticed her face and dress were covered in yellow mango juice.

"Dandelion," I said.

"What, what?" said my mother.

"Nothing," I said.

It was early bathtime for us that day. Very early. In the bathroom my mother never stopped scolding. "You know what?" she said. "Your name shouldn't be Melanie Treble at all. I've a good mind to change it to Melanie Trouble. And since I don't want any more trouble, there'll be no more playing outside for the rest of the day."

Sitting at the table that afternoon I

thought, "Since I can't go out and play I'll make my pencil and crayons do the playing for me."

First I drew Flora as a dandelion. Then I drew myself as a hibiscus. Next I drew my great-grandma on all fours and Flora and me taking turns to have a piggyback.

I was having so much fun, I got quite carried away and sketched a lovely machine gun. Of course I didn't dare give it a name in case my mum saw it. I couldn't leave my father out so he was a tall tree.

When all the drawings were finished, I wrote Melanie Trouble on the bottom of the picture. Then I scratched it out and wrote Melanie Treble.

Flora poked her head in the door with a grin as bright as a sunflower.

"Melanie," she whispered.

"What do you want now?" I said.

"I've planted the two mango seeds right under our bedroom window. When they grow into trees there'll be one whole tree for me and one for you."

"Good on you," I laughed.

According to Poppa, he was the only person in the world who appreciated cheese.

THE CHEESE PARTY

Now let me tell you about the time Flora and I persuaded our father to share fair with the cheese. Cheese was the most favourite food of the family but Poppa gave us very little of it.

"Did you see that big piece of cheese Poppa just ate, Mel?"

"With cheese Poppa thinks BIG but only for himself. He eats it in hunks: breakfast, dinner, teatime, any time. You know that, Flora."

"Not fair. He should give us bigger pieces and not eat it all up like that."

"Tell him, then," I said.

"Uh-huh, not me," said Flora. "I don't

want to learn any more about the stuff, I just want to eat it."

Flora was right. She and I had to endure lectures on the quality of a piece of cheese and how it was made, generally with obscure facts about the cheeses of the world thrown in. We were expected to remember every thing Poppa told us and fire the facts right back at him.

"Who was Aristaeus?" he would ask.

"Son of Apollo," we'd reply.

"And what had Aristaeus to do with cheese?"

"The Greek god of cheese, Poppa."

"Right," he'd say. "You can see how important cheese was to the ancient Greeks. And what was good enough for them is good enough for me."

And after all this, what did we get?

A tiny fragment of cheese.

"Real meanie," we'd grumble. "Wasn't worth waiting for."

According to Poppa, he was the only person in the world who appreciated cheese. Whenever my mother offered to go and buy some, his answer was always the same. "Perish the thought. Choosing cheese is a serious business. A chooser of cheese has to have know-how and in this house that's me."

"There's more to cheese than eating it," he would say, popping a piece in his mouth. If he described it as "flaky from Wales", Flora and I guessed it to be Caerphilly; if he said "sunburst yellow and mellow texture", we shouted "Cheddar". His description of Italian Parmesan gave us the giggles. "It's one of the hardest cheeses about," he'd say. "You can leave a tooth or two behind if you don't watch out."

Once he brought home a cheese which had great holes in it like craters. He handled it as if it were a piece of my mother's best china.

"Fromage," he said, with a great grin on his face.

"Fromage," we said.

"French," he said. "The word for cheese in French."

"Fromage is the word for cheese in French," we recited, hoping that this new piece of information would bring us future rewards.

"And listen to this," continued Poppa. "The French have a cheese for every day of the year. Can you believe that?"

"Never, Poppa," we said.

"You better believe it," he said.

Flora and I liked tasting times best. This was when Poppa set out several cheeses on the table and tasted them one after the other. His exaggerated praises would accompany each bite: "Hmmm … lovely! This is like riding on the crest of a wave … and this is like a piece of heaven … good for body and soul … if you haven't tasted this flavour you haven't lived."

During tasting times we always hoped to get a good sized piece of cheese. Sometimes we did, but hoping and getting are often two entirely different things.

"Poppa won't share fair and we must do something about it," I said to Flora one day.

"Help ourselves."

"We'll be caught."

"Don't be silly. We'll be so smart Poppa won't notice a thing."

From then on we started taking matters into our own hands – or fingers, to be exact. No piece of cheese escaped if it was lying around looking as if it wouldn't be missed by anyone.

At first we barely nipped the edges. Soon little nips turned into big pieces. Then we got carried away and took too much. Poppa noticed.

"Who's been eating my cheese?"

"Nobody, Poppa," we'd reply sharply. And for days after we'd leave the cheese alone.

"Who wants his little old cheese anyway?" we'd grumble to ourselves. But the moment we thought it safe we started all over again.

"My fair share," I said as I took a piece.

"And my fair share, too," said Flora, plunking a piece in her mouth.

Our father kept right on giving us see-through slices but it didn't matter any more. Flora and I would exchange looks which meant, "We know what we know and if you knew what we know you wouldn't give us any more cheese at all."

Then one evening, when we least expected it, my father came charging into the room.

"Who's been eating my cheeses again?" he asked.

My heart skipped a beat. Flora squeaked, "Oweee!"

"Who's been eating my cheeses again?" repeated my father.

"Nobody, Poppa," we chorused.

"But it was nobody who did it the last time and the time before that too," said my father. "This nobody should ask before taking and if he takes before asking that's pinching and nobody pinches my cheese and gets away with it."

My mother came in.

"This nobody business is a whole lot of

nonsense," she said. "I blame the mice myself."

"Mice!" said my father. "Impossible."

"Can't you see they're waltzing off with chunks of your cheese? Stockpiling their larder no doubt," said my mother.

"Right then," said my father. "It's time we showed these mice who's boss around here."

"I agree," said my mother. "But how will you do it?"

"This is a problem for the whole family to solve," said my father.

Flora and I shuffled on the sofa. We sat tightly together trying to put as much space as possible between us and our parents.

"Any suggestions, Flora, on how to get rid of mice?" asked my father.

"Eee." Flora made a mousy kind of sound before she said, "A cat, Poppa."

"And you, Melanie?" asked my father.

"Any suggestions on how to get rid of mice?"
asked my father.

"A cat," I agreed.

"Good thinking," said my father. "But these are clever mice and it would take a whole cattery of cats to do the job properly."

"What about setting a trap, then?" said my mother with the tiniest smile at the corner of her mouth.

"You mean a mouse-trap?" said my father.

"Exactly."

"Good idea." said my father. "Now why didn't I think of that? When a mouse smells a nice piece of my best cheese he'll certainly have to take a nibble. And then the trap will come down like this … SNAP!"

My father made such a big noise as he brought down one large palm on the other that Flora and I nearly jumped out of our skins.

"Let's own up," whispered Flora.

"Shut up, silly," I whispered back.

That night Flora and I stood by our bedroom window. We gazed up at the bright, full moon gliding across the night sky. It looked like the biggest, roundest, yellowest cheese escaping before our very eyes.

"Can the man in the moon eat as much cheese as he wants to, Melanie?" asked Flora.

"Who knows?" I said.

"Please, Mr Moon, send some moonbeams down with lots of cheeses for us. That way we can have our very own cheesery in our bedroom," said Flora.

"That's a big wish," I said.

"Do Momma and Poppa really think mice are pinching the cheese?" asked Flora, looking as if she knew the answer already.

"They're on to us, I think. But I can't understand why they're pretending they think it's mice," I said.

"I'm going to tell Poppa the truth tomorrow," said Flora.

"What! And put the blame on me? You mustn't," I said.

"I won't blame you, Melanie."

"Leave things as they are, Flora," I warned.

Next day my father told us he was going to have a cheese party that evening.

"Why?" I asked. "Is it your birthday?"

"No. I just feel like having a good time," said my father.

"How many guests are coming, Poppa?" I asked.

"Enough," said my father. "A couple of neighbours maybe."

"That doesn't sound like a lot of people," said Flora.

"Shhh, silly," I whispered. "Too many guests will gobble up all the cheese. None will be left for us."

All that day our parents behaved very strangely. They kept whispering to each other and laughing more than usual. But we didn't pay much attention. We were too excited about the cheese party.

"Just think of it," said Flora. "A kitchenful of cheese right under our noses."

But we were sent off to bed early that evening.

"They're so mean," Flora sulked.

"Spoilsports," I said. "Let's take a peep anyway."

"Poppa and Momma will be angry."

"They won't know a thing if we're quiet. Just a little peep before we get into bed."

The kitchen door opened easily and we tiptoed in. I noticed a large piece of Cheddar first.

"Your wish is granted, Flora," I said. "Look, a slice of the moon has parked itself right in the middle of the table."

But Flora was gazing at a red, round, velvety cheese.

"Guess this riddle, Mel," she said.

"What riddle?"

"I look like a red ball. But I'm not for kicking so I must be for eating. What am I?"

"I'm Edam, I am," I said.

Flora giggled.

"Wonderful cheese," I said. "Lovely smells."

Flora pinched a piece of Caerphilly. "Tastes even better," she said, popping it into her mouth. Then she went on, mimicking my father: "Creamy on the tongue… Hmmm, a piece of heaven."

I pinched a bit too and after this there was no stopping us. We went from cheese to cheese: Double Gloucester, Barrel, Dry Jack, Stilton, Lancashire, Deadman's Head and many more.

"Taste this one, Flora. It's delicious."

"What is it?"

"Wensleydale. Poppa says that it's the grandfather of all cheese. Long ago monks used to make it from ewes' milk."

"There's a strange one here," said Flora. "But I don't like the look of it. It has stringy, blue-black, wormy, wiggling things all through it."

I sniffed it. "It doesn't half pong."

Then Flora sniffed it. "Yuck. It smells like Uncle Fred's toes when he takes off his shoes."

We collapsed with the giggles. Then I said,

"I wonder what it tastes like."

"Yuck. I don't fancy tasting Uncle Fred's cheesy toes," said Flora.

We giggled all over again until the tears rolled down our cheeks.

Then I saw the name – GORGONZOLA. "Poppa always talks about it. He says it's so rich and the smell is so powerful it could walk out of the fridge if it had a mind to."

"Gorgonzola," said Flora slowly. "I like that name. I can even beat a rhythm to it. Gor-gon-zo-la."

Soon Flora and I were dancing around the table chanting, "Gor-gon-zo-la hold your nose! I won't taste you, not in the least. Gor-gon-zo-la smelly cheese, makes me think of Uncle's toes!"

And all the while we kept stuffing pieces of cheese into our mouths.

"I must try this one and this and this,"

Flora shouted, darting from cheese to cheese.

"Shush," I said. "You're making too much noise. And look what you've done, Flora. You've taken too much. Poppa is bound to notice."

"No, I haven't. What about you? You ate all that French one. That's greedy."

When we got thirsty we poured ourselves a glass of sarsaparilla.

"It's only the two of us, but it seems like a real party," I said.

"It's fun," said Flora.

Just then we heard our parents' voices and we scarpered.

The next morning I woke up pretty early. I felt a queasiness in my stomach and started to toss and turn and moan. Flora was moaning too.

Not long after that we both charged for the

It was the first of many trips.

bathroom and nearly got stuck together in the doorway. It was the first of many trips.

"What's wrong, Melanie and Flora?" asked my mother. "You seem to be taking up residence in the bathroom today."

"I don't feel so good, Momma," whined Flora.

Coming out of the bathroom for the umpteenth time, Flora and I came face to face with our parents. They each held a spoonful of medicine.

"Swallow this," they said. "It'll stop you to-ing and fro-ing."

By the afternoon Flora and I were all right again. Then came suppertime.

"I'm feeling generous today. VEEERY GENEROUS," Poppa said. "How big a slice do you want, Melanie?"

"Ugh. No cheese for me today, Poppa.

Thanks," I said.

"Maybe you'd rather have a piece of Stilton, the king of cheeses?" said my father.

"No thanks."

"How about you, Flora?"

"No thanks, Poppa," said Flora, making an awful grimace.

"Well now," said my father, scratching his head. "I never thought I'd see the day when you girls refused a piece of cheese!"

"I don't believe it," said my mother.

Both our parents had a strange look on their faces. Like foxes up to mischief. We had a funny feeling there was more to come so we stayed quiet and waited.

A few seconds later Poppa said, "By the way, that little problem with the mice: don't worry your pretty little heads about it any more."

"Don't worry?" we said.

"No need," said my father with a funny laugh in his throat.

"No need," repeated my mother, nursing a strange smile.

"You'll be glad to know that your mother and I have caught them fair and square," my father went on.

Flora and I felt like two cornered mice with no safe hole to scuttle into.

"You caught the mice?" I asked.

"You bet. Two of them," said my father, laughing way down in his stomach.

"But they got away with a mighty lot of cheese. I hope it didn't make them ill from eating too much," said my mother and she started to laugh right along with my father.

"And we didn't have to use any cats either," said my father.

My parents laughed and laughed until tears came to their eyes. By now even Flora twigged that the joke was on us and that we were the two guests at my father's cheese party. Yes, they'd set a trap for us and we'd walked straight into it.

Then after what seemed like a very long time, my parents wiped their eyes and stopped laughing. But only long enough for my father to say, "Yes sirree, you could say that catching those mice was like catching a duck with one grain of corn." And this made them laugh all over again.

"They're behaving like two spoilt kids," I thought.

Then my father held his nose and said, "Gor-gon-zo-la, hold your nose…"

We felt uncomfortable at first, and then we saw the funny side.

Smiling with us, Poppa said, "Well, girls, by now you will have learnt that you can have too much of a good thing. Even something as nice as cheese. And I've learnt something also."

"You have?" Flora and I chorused.

"Oh yes. From now on I shall share fair," he said. "I've learnt that I'm not the only one who likes cheese in this family."

Flora and I laughed right along with our parents.

"The way I see it, that's a BIG job you got there,"
said Flora.

FATHER CHRISTMAS RIDES A SKATEBOARD

One morning my mother handed me a pile of freshly washed laundry.

"Fold these up neatly, Melanie," she said. "And make sure that you roll the socks into pairs."

"I'll never finish this on time," I moaned as soon as my mother left the room.

"On time for what?" asked an idle Flora.

"On time to try out Murve's new skateboard. That's what, nosy."

"He's gone out," said Flora.

"Don't be silly. I mean when he comes back from shopping with his mom."

Murve's my friend. He lives next door.

We're the same age and we get along just fine provided Flora doesn't muck things up for us.

Flora gave a deep sigh. "The way I see it, that's a BIG job you got there. That's an all day job so I guess I'll have to try out Murve's skateboard for you," she said cheekily.

"No, you won't. See you stay away from us. You always spoil our games when you're around."

"You're always mean to me," said Flora.

"I'm never mean to you but you are to me, otherwise you'd help me fold these clothes."

"No way," said Flora sharply. "I've my own things to do."

"Like what?"

"Like writing to Father Christmas and drawing a huge picture of him to hang on my bedroom wall."

"Don't be daft, Flora. You can't do that

now. Christmas is a long, long way away."

"It isn't a long, long way away. December is only the month after next and Christmas is actually in eight weeks and four days' time and it falls on a Wednesday. I checked it, so there!" said Flora in one breath.

Flora was being Flora, yet again. When she was losing an argument she always tried to cover it up by blinding me with newly acquired facts.

"Please yourself," I said. "So long as you don't bother me, OK?"

"I won't," said Flora and she began writing her letter to Father Christmas.

Flora couldn't spell but she had a look on her face which said, I'm not going to let a little thing like that come between me and Father Christmas, not one bit. But I knew she was going to ask for help. I started to hum. I glanced at her every now and then.

"Help me, Mel," she said after a while. "You're such a good speller."

"Oh no, Flora. You won't get around me that way."

"Could you write Dear Father Christmas for me?"

"Fair's fair," I said. "You won't help me, I won't help you either."

Without warning Flora ran into the kitchen. "Please, Momma," she whined. "Can you write Dear Father Christmas for me, 'cause I asked Mel and she won't help me."

From the kitchen my mother's voice came booming out. "Melanie, can't you see I'm busy? Help your little sister, you hear me?"

Flora came back into the room with the biggest grin of triumph on her face. I felt like knocking paper and pencil to the ground and trampling on them.

Instead I said, "I hope you know that Father Christmas won't like it when he finds you didn't write this letter yourself."

"Who's going to tell him?"

"I didn't say anybody'll tell him, did I? He has ways and means of finding these things out, silly."

Flora cocked her head on one side like Daisy, my pet chicken. I could almost hear her thinking.

"I know how to get around that," she said after a few minutes. "You write the letter on a different piece of paper, then I'll copy it in my own handwriting on to mine."

"No, Flora, I'll spell the words you can't spell but you'll do all the writing."

Flora finished her letter just as I rolled the last pair of socks.

"That's it," I told her. "No more help from me today."

"Don't need your help. I can draw Father Christmas all by myself, so there!" she said and immediately started to stick two sheets of paper together.

It was then I heard Murve shouting, "Coming down, Mel?"

"You bet," I shouted back.

Before I dashed down the stairs I gave Flora a strong warning.

"Listen to me, Flora. And listen well. You keep your Father Christmas to yourself. And stay up here, you hear?"

At first I had to watch Murve gliding up and down the pavement a few times.

"I'm breaking it in gently," he told me.

He showed me how to flip the skateboard just before a turn in order to land properly and keep your balance at the same time. Afterwards we started to take turns.

When it was Murve's turn for the third

*Murve showed me how to flip the skateboard
just before a turn.*

time, he whizzed past me like the wind and when he reached the corner of the street he spun round and started to skate back with his arms spread out like an eagle.

Too late I saw Flora running across Murve's path with her sheets of paper trailing behind her. She wasn't looking where she was going.

"Look, Mel," she shouted. "I've finished drawing Father Christmas."

"Get out … get out of the way!" I screamed, but in vain. There was a noisy bump as Murve swerved and jumped off the pavement in order to avoid hitting Flora. He missed her but had to skate on quite a way before he stopped with his arms around a lamppost and the Father Christmas wrapped around his legs.

Flora screamed as she watched her precious Father Christmas trying to have a go on the skateboard.

"My Father Christmas! My Father Christmas!" cried Flora, running after Murve.

"Dumb kid," muttered Murve as he tried to untangle himself.

"It's all mashed up," howled Flora, gathering bits of the torn picture.

She pushed the pieces towards me. "Put it together, please."

"Put it together yourself, stupid Father Christmas," I snapped and knocked the paper from her hand. "You're lucky Murve is so good on the skateboard."

"It's not my fault," sobbed Flora. "It's Murve's."

"Sorry, Flora. I couldn't help it," said Murve, as he picked up the pieces of paper and handed her the head and arms of Father Christmas, which he tried to smooth out.

*Flora threw her head back and
opened her mouth wide.*

Then he looked at his dirty hands and said, "I must go. See you later."

Flora went on crying. She had mucked up our game and yet she was the one who was making all the fuss. I was furious.

"Anyway, there's no Father Christmas. That's all baby stuff." I blurted out.

That did it! Oh boy! Flora threw her head back and opened her mouth wide. I could see the back of her throat. She let out a piercing scream, shattering my ear drums and, judging by what happened next, shattering the heavens. Instantly the sun pulled its head in behind the clouds and the sky grumbled, trying hard to drown out Flora's noise. Then it started to rain buckets.

This day and me feel the same, I thought. Very angry!

I ran upstairs and straight to my bedroom. Flora went dripping and bawling to the kitchen. I could hear her wailing as she tittle-tattled to my mother.

"Trouble always seems to follow me," I thought.

And then the rain stopped as sharply as it had started. The sun came beaming out again and I felt it was having a good laugh at me.

"You can beam all over your face," I told the sun from my window. "It's all right for you. You're safe up there."

A few minutes later Flora's crying stopped. I didn't even hear a sniffle.

Any minute now my mother is bound to shout for me, I thought. But she didn't. I wondered what was happening. Soon I got so curious I had to check things out. I left the room and walked bravely to the kitchen door.

I stopped and listened for a bit. Hearing

nothing, I put one foot in the door and then the other, and sidled in like a crab.

My mother's back was turned as she handed Flora a small dish of ice-cream. Flora looked up and saw me.

"Piggy-Wiggy," I mouthed.

"Momma, Melanie's making faces at me," cried Flora.

I scarpered.

"Your father will deal with you later, Melanie," my mother called.

My father's newspaper seemed to have ten times more news in it that day and he kept making angry rustling noises turning the pages.

Flora sat beside him with a look on her face which said: "You're in big trouble, Melanie, and it serves you right."

I stared at her, thinking, "Lucky you're

not near me or I'd pinch you like I was a crab with claws."

But I wished I could take back what I had told her about Father Christmas.

I wondered why my father was taking so long to say something. My mother must have read my thoughts because she cleared her throat and gave him a look. He folded the newspaper and put it away.

"Now, Melanie," said my father. "Is it true that you said what Flora told me, that you told her about Father Christmas? I hope you understand the question. I put it this way because I don't like to repeat hearsay."

"I understand," I said, though the way my father put this question made it sound more like a riddle than a regular question.

I didn't answer right away. I needed more thinking time.

Meanwhile Flora sniffled softly at first,

"Let's put the record straight once and for all,"
said my father.

then louder and louder.

"My Father Christmas is all torn up and soggy," she blabbered. "I can't stick it back together and it's Murve's fault and Melanie said that there's no Father Christmaaaaaas!"

"Enough now, Flora," said my father.

Flora calmed down immediately. While I was thinking what a clever actress she's going to be when she grows up, my father was patiently waiting for my reply.

"Let me put the question another way," he said. "Did you not tell Flora that her picture of Father Christmas wasn't the real thing?"

"That's what I *meant*," I heard myself saying. "But I was upset and the words didn't come out the right way." It was a little fib but it was the only answer I could give.

"I expect you're a little wiser now, Melanie," said my father. "Now you know that in order to make your words come out right you should always think first and when you're upset give yourself even more thinking time. Understand?"

"Yes, Poppa," I said.

But Flora, who always needed everything to be as simple as ABC, still wasn't satisfied.

"Tell Melanie that there's a real Father Christmas and that he isn't any baby stuff, Poppa," she insisted.

"Let's put the record straight once and for all," said my father. "And since I'd like to put a smile back on your face, Flora, I suggest that we play a little game. I'll ask you three questions and I want you to answer True or False. Agreed?"

"Yes," said Flora.

"ONE: Father is a word you know quite well. TRUE or FALSE?"

"True!" shouted Flora.

"TWO: There's a festival called

Christmas which we celebrate on the 25th December. TRUE or FALSE?"

"True!" shouted Flora, smiling.

"THREE: Melanie and Flora are loving sisters who receive many presents from Father Christmas each year. TRUE or FALSE?"

"True!" both of us shouted.

"Well, Flora, you got all three questions right. Isn't that something?"

"Yes, Poppa," said Flora.

"You're a clever girl to work out things for yourself," my father said and Flora was all smiles.

It was then that Murve returned with a large, long sheet of paper.

"You can draw another Father Christmas. An even bigger and better one," he said, handing the paper to Flora.

"I'll help you to draw it whenever you're

ready," I offered.

"But please, please," pleaded Murve, "don't let Father Christmas ever again try to have a go on my skateboard."

Flora laughed.

"And don't forget," said my father, "when you're ready, give me your letter to Father Christmas, and I'll post it."

"I'm thinking about her lovely jewellery."

SHARE AND SHARE ALIKE

"Flora, guess what! Only three days to go," I said, pointing at the calendar.

"Yum-yum," said Flora. "Only three days to wait for Aunt Stella's scrumptious cakes."

"I'm thinking about her lovely jewellery. When I grow up I shall have lots and lots. Just like her."

"Oh, Melanie, jewellery is silly. What can you do with rings, chains and bangles? They can only glitter and jangle."

"I like beautiful things. That's what."

"I don't. You can't eat them. Give me cakes and sweets any time."

"No matter," I said. "We have to get there

first – and remember what happened last month?"

"Nothing."

"How right you are. Nothing did happen. We didn't go because you squealed out like a scalded pig."

"You pulled my hair."

"That'll teach you not to tell on me. One day you'll tell one tale too many and your tongue will get as long as Pinocchio's nose."

Flora pushed her tongue out at me and I did the same back to her. Then we started to make the most awful faces at each other.

"Stop that nonsense, Melanie and Flora," said my mother, looking up from her sewing. "Another stunt like that and you won't be going to Aunt Stella's. Is that quite clear?"

"Yes, Momma," we chorused.

I must keep out of trouble for three whole days, I thought to myself. Very tricky. You see, trouble had a strange way of keeping me company.

I did *try*. "Get thee behind me, Satan," I used to say. But it didn't always work, and I would find myself facing my mother's angry wagging finger and fire-spitting words.

But Saturday came at last. And although I couldn't remember getting into any trouble, I held my breath.

"Your aunt is expecting us early, so move sharp, girls," said my mother, at breakfast.

"Magic," I thought, and breathed again.

Flora was the first dressed. She sat down as still as a doorstop while my mother put two enormous bows in her hair, which fanned out on either side of her head like a pair of swan's wings.

Then it was my turn. When my mother had finished my last plait she said, "That looks real neat, Mel. Mind you keep it that way. And remember to behave yourself at your aunt's."

"I will, Momma," I said. And I really meant it.

"I always behave. Don't I, Momma?" chipped in Flora smugly.

"Nearly always, my flower," said my mother, giving her a warm smile.

The little creep, I thought to myself. The limelight stealer. Flora hated it when she wasn't up front with my mother and I hated her for stealing my mother's attention from me. I snarled at her. She glowered back.

Momma left the room.

"Why do you have to put your little two cents' worth in?" I hissed. "Momma wasn't speaking to you."

"So what?"

"You're a little meddler. That's what," I said.

"The little creep," I thought to myself.

"I'm not a meddler. My name's Flora."

"My leetle flower," I said, mimicking my mother. "Meddling flower. Meddling flower."

"Momma, Melanie's calling me names," shouted Flora, far too loud for comfort.

As she opened her mouth to shout again, I clamped my hands over it and her voice tapered away.

"Don't be such a goof!" I said. "Remember what happened last time."

My mother came back.

"What's going on?" she said, looking suspiciously at us.

"Nothing," I said quickly.

"Nothing," echoed Flora.

"Let's be off then," said Momma.

"Phew! A near miss," I thought. "Get thee behind me, Satan."

As always, the smells coming from Aunt Stella's kitchen were out of this world.

Sniffing the air like a puppy, Flora called out, "Cinnamon, vanilla, lemon."

Not to be outdone I joined in with, "Grated orange peel, burnt sugar and almond."

Inside, the smells of essences, fruits and spices got stronger and stronger. They wrapped themselves around us and tickled our nostrils before twirling through the warm air and floating up to the ceiling where they lingered for quite some time. I could've sworn I heard encircling whispers of "Welcome, welcome."

Slowly, we took in the display of cakes, pastries and homemade sweets. There were gooey coconut tarts and powder buns baked to a golden colour, filled with raisins and spiced with nutmeg and vanilla. There were pumpkin pies, banana cakes, biscuits baked crispy and flaky, and tarts piled high with gorgeous fillings. On a shelf by themselves sat the larger cakes dripping with chocolate, fresh cream and molasses, while the sweets and candies were displayed in colourful glass jars. Those were for Aunt Stella's shop.

Aunt Stella gave us a large piece of our favourite candy. It was made from lemon juice and molasses. It was a caramelly colour and stretched like a piece of elastic. "Stretch-me-guts" was our special name for it.

We took one end each and started pulling. We pulled and pulled and the candy stretched and stretched. The middle got thinner and thinner till it made a popping noise like a soft balloon. We each took our half, rolled it into a snail, and sucked away to our hearts' content.

Then came the highlight of the afternoon. Teatime.

As Aunt Stella uncovered the table with a great flourish, her many bangles tinkled magically.

"Abracadabra," I said. And there appeared a banquet fit for princesses.

"Yum-yum," said Flora and we both tucked in.

I dived for my favourites first and soon my mouth was chock-full of coconut tarts.

Flora built a great pyramid out of one or two of everything on the table. We didn't talk unless you counted the murmurs of *ooh*, *aah* and *lovely*.

I finished first and looked around at the others. Flora was still eating as if she was racing against the clock. Momma and my aunt were having a whale of a time talking. They slapped each other on the shoulders.

Oh, the ornaments! The jewels!...
I gazed, spellbound.

They screamed out when they exchanged a juicy bit of news. Sometimes they laughed so much real tears came to their eyes. But they just wiped them away and started all over again.

They weren't paying me a blind bit of notice, so I did my disappearing act.

I stood in front of the dressing table in Aunt Stella's bedroom. Oh, the ornaments! The jewels! Zillions of them and every one beautiful and glittering. The musical box with the porcelain ballerina on top was right in the middle of the table and I could see its reflection in the mirror. I gazed, spellbound. "Mind you look but don't touch," said a little voice in my head.

I heard it but my hands didn't. They shot out in front of me and picked up the musical box. Then my fingers started to wind the key round and round. When the ballerina began to dance I forgot about Flora, Momma and Aunt Stella. I forgot where I was and who I was. To add to the enchantment the sun's rays streaked through the window and everything began to twinkle and shimmer. The rings and bracelets and necklaces came alive. They had voices like wind chimes.

Choose me. I'm pretty. And me. Wear me just for a few minutes. Please.

Now they were invitations I couldn't refuse.

First, I slipped on a few bangles and then I added another and another till my arm looked just like Aunt Stella's, whose bangles started from her wrist and ended up just below her elbow.

There was no turning back now. I chose the most brilliant pieces of jewellery:

earrings, gold chains, necklaces and rings for each finger.

I looked in the mirror, and to my amazement a beauty princess in the Carnival Parade gazed back at me. When I'd had enough of her I quickly changed to a film star. There was the flash-flashing of bulbs as photographers kept on snap-snapping.

I posed this way and that. I smiled. I preened. And afterwards I signed autographs for my fans.

I wound up the musical box again and this time I was transformed into Cinderella. I danced with the prince at the ball. My earrings tinkled. My bangles jingled. Just like Aunt Stella's.

Then the midnight hour struck. But there was no fairy godmother – it was Aunt Stella and she sounded just like one of the ugly sisters.

"MELANIEEEEEE! What the deuce are you doing in my bedroom? I told you never to play around with my jewellery, you naughty, naughty girl!" she screeched. It was blood-curdling. All the neighbours heard. And right along the street, through their windows and out of their doors, they poked their heads.

Meanwhile, Aunt Stella reclaimed her jewellery. She was very thorough. It was one earring out followed by a whack on my arm. Then the other earring out, and another whack. Frankly, I was so scared I didn't feel a thing.

The bangles came off pretty easily but my aunt had difficulty with the necklace. She yanked and yanked. But it got stuck in the hook half of the hook-and-eye fastener at the back of my dress, then snapped. Dozens of pearly beads clattered to the floor, spilling

Aunt Stella yanked and yanked at the necklace.

back and forth like waves around our feet.

I felt as if I was in the middle of a white, foamy ocean and I prayed for a huge wave to come crashing over me. My mother came instead. Saved at last! I thought.

But when I looked up into her face I wasn't so sure. There was fire in her eyes and her lips were trembling. We left my aunt's quicker than bullets being fired from a gun.

When we got home my father was reading on the sofa. He looked like a newspaper with crossed legs.

I headed for my bedroom. From there I could hear my mother telling him what had happened. My father listened. I heard him folding his paper before he put it away.

My mother talked. Stopped. Talked some more. My father cleared his throat and grunted something I couldn't quite catch.

Then everything was quiet. I had time to think. I told myself that Aunt Stella was OK most of the time. She was kind and she would give us almost anything we wanted but she hated us kids going into her bedroom and mucking about with her things. Since I knew this I had to admit I was in the wrong.

"You'll cop it now," said Flora.

"Shush," I snapped.

"You'll be whipped into next week," she went on gleefully.

"Want to bet?" My words were brave but my inside was all jelly.

"You will. You will." Flora kept up the taunting like a she-devil. "Six of the best. That's what you'll get."

"How do you know, Miss Know-all?" I said.

"I just know," said Flora.

I had to think of something to shut her up.

"Smacks are OK by me," I said, bluffing it out. "I'd sooner have that than nag, nag, nag."

"You mean to tell me you can stand six smacks?" asked Flora.

"I don't remember saying that I'll get six," I said.

"But you will."

"Oh, no I won't. Only last week I gave you two of those dolls Mrs Buckley gave me for doing her shopping. Momma told me to. Remember? 'Share and share alike in this house,' she said."

"That's different."

"Haa-haa," I said. "No difference. You won't wiggle out of this one so easy."

"Haa-haa to you too. I don't even like jewellery and I didn't break Aunt Stella's

86

necklace."

"Just wait and see, Flora."

After supper my father sat down between Flora and me. Flora quickly got up.

"Going somewhere special, Flora?" asked my father.

"I forgot something, Poppa," said Flora.

"I'll be right here when you get back," said my father. A few seconds later Flora returned and threw her two dolls into my lap. "You can have them back," she said.

"What's going on here?" asked my father, scooping up the dolls in his huge hand.

"Melanie said that it's share and share alike and if I share her dolls I have to share her smackings and I don't want to be smacked," said Flora in one long breath and then burst out crying.

"Hold on a minute," said my father.

"I wouldn't like to have to give away six of my best,"
said my father.

"Melanie, Flora. Something bothering you? Would you like to tell me about it?"

"Not me, Poppa," said Flora, sniffling. "But Melanie would."

"I hope the news is good. I wouldn't like to have to give away six of my best," said my father, examining his huge open hands.

"It was all Melanie's fault," said Flora, bawling with all her might. She stopped to catch her breath, then she bawled all over again in a different key.

"The orchestra's tuning up for real," said my father. "Shush! Let's have some quiet."

Flora's bawling changed to a sniffle. She put her hands over her face and peeped through her open fingers.

My father sat back on the sofa, wrinkling his brow and screwing up his eyes so that you could only see the glint in them.

"Well now, I heard that you created an

almighty din at your aunt's, Melanie. Want to tell me about it?" His voice sounded deep down in his slippers. I swallowed.

While I was still thinking how best to tell my side of the story, Flora broke the silence.

"What's create?" she asked.

I could've hugged her. I wished she would go on and on asking questions until my father had forgotten he'd asked me one.

"Create means to develop something, to…"

But before he could finish, Flora shouted, "Melanie didn't create anything. She broke Aunt Stella's best pearl necklace. And wasn't Aunt Stella angry! Oh boy!"

I glared at Flora. "I didn't break the necklace," I said.

"You *didn't*?" said my father in a very dramatic way.

"Yes … no … I mean, Aunt Stella broke it

herself. She pulled too hard, Poppa," I said.

"And Aunt Stella nearly yanked Melanie's neck off too," said Flora.

My father got up. Putting his hands behind his back he began rocking back and forth on his heels. "So you admit to going into your aunt's room knowing full well that it's against the rules?"

"Yes," I said in my meekest voice.

"You also admit to wearing her precious jewellery?"

"Yes," I said.

"Now I want you to think well before answering the next question," said my father. "The deed is done. You've had time enough to think about it. What promise can you make to show that you have learnt your lesson?"

I took my father at his word and I wasn't in any hurry to give an answer. But Flora thought it best to fill up the silence.

"You mean to say Melanie will get away without any punishment?" she said.

I looked daggers at her and if my father hadn't been there I'd have yanked both the swan's wings from her hair.

"Let's examine the situation carefully, Flora," said my father. He held up three fingers.

"One, Melanie was told off by her aunt. You said so yourself." Flora nodded.

"Two, she had her neck nearly yanked off. You said that too." Flora nodded again.

"Three, she was smacked on her arm more than once. I call that a whooooole lot of punishment. Don't you?" My father paused for Flora to answer.

"Well. Don't you?" he prompted.

"That's a whooooole lot of punishment," repeated Flora.

"Good," said my father. "And now we must give Melanie a chance to speak for herself."

"I don't ever want to see any earrings, bangles or necklaces ever again. Never, never," I said.

"And how do you suppose you'll manage that?" asked my father. "Turn your head every time you pass a jeweller's shop window? Close your eyes whenever you see your aunt? Or maybe you intend to stop visiting her, eh?"

"Nooooooo!" screeched Flora when she heard the last remark.

"Hold on, Flora. Hold on," said my father. "I want to hear what Melanie has to say."

"I'll never go into Aunt Stella's bedroom and put on her jewellery again," I said under my breath.

"Speak up," said my father.

I did.

"That's more like it. That's a promise you can keep," my father said, nodding his head vigorously.

"Next time Melanie should stay in the kitchen with me," suggested Flora.

"Great," said my father. "Then she can munch through a whooooole lot of cakes. Just like you. Are you sure there'll be enough for both of you?"

Flora giggled. And once she realized that the threat of a smacking wasn't hanging over her any more, she scooped up the two dolls from the sofa.

"Share and share alike still stands," she said.

THE

END

Any Waking Morning

The publisher gratefully acknowledges the support of the Canada Council for the Arts and the Ontario Arts Council. The publisher is also grateful for the financial assistance received from the Government of Canada.

Front cover artwork: J. Davidson-Palmer, "Tao: The Path to Good Fortune," 2005, acrylic on canvas, 16 x 16 inches. Copyright © J. Davidson-Palmer. Website: www.judithdavidsonpalmer.com

Library and Archives Canada Cataloguing in Publication

Title: Any waking morning : poems / Mary Lou Soutar-Hynes.
Names: Soutar-Hynes, Mary Lou, author.
Series: Inanna poetry & fiction series.
Description: Series statement: Inanna Poetry & Fiction Series
Identifiers: Canadiana (print) 20190094133 | Canadiana (ebook) 20190094141 | ISBN 9781771336413 (softcover) | ISBN 9781771336420 (epub) | ISBN 9781771336437 (Kindle) | ISBN 9781771336444 (pdf)
Classification: LCC PS8587.O9756 A69 2019 | DDC C811/.6—dc23

Printed and bound in Canada

Inanna Publications and Education Inc.
210 Founders College, York University
4700 Keele Street, Toronto, Ontario M3J 1P3 Canada
Telephone: (416) 736–5356   Fax (416) 736–5765
Email: inanna.publications@inanna.ca Website: www.inanna.ca

MIX
Paper from
responsible sources
FSC® C004071

ALSO BY MARY LOU SOUTAR-HYNES

Dark Water Songs
Travelling Light
The Fires of Naming

Any Waking Morning

poems by
Mary Lou Soutar-Hynes

inanna poetry & fiction series

INANNA Publications and Education Inc.
Toronto, Canada

for Anne-Marie

Contents

III: Beyond Convergence

IV: Fragments and Heartwood

I. The Way the Light Falls

In Matters of Art

Everywhere a poem —
voiced and unspoken,   those overlapping
layers,   degrees of separation

Unintended intersections,   random phrase,   tectonic
plates and truth's scale   darkly sliding —
call   of great grey owl

One small spider
weaves her web across the page
tentative as light —
sub-text and punctuation   holding us together —
gravity,   meaning's cloud

This universe of unseen commas our only certainty
photons wandering weightless —
at will

A Question of Flowering

The seeds of poems scatter
randomly as ragweed   on warm August days

a T-Shirt   proclaiming
Next Stop
PARA
DISE

just subtle colour,   no hint
of requirements —
visa,   inoculations,   how to get there —
perhaps its owner has deeper insights
into transit

the sandalled,   grey-clad
nun on the 53A   taking the only vacant seat
so nun and ex-nun   are side-by-side
Westbound —
her mention of sweet violets,   foxglove
rosemary

a flowering of images
planted in the mind till you succumb,   resort
to text —   that never-ending   pruning
fine-tuning —
density's weight   on edge and line,   fluid
evocations,   ceaseless
merging —   shadow's lyric declinations
            marking altitudes
                of sun

Musings on the Lakeshore Line

i.   *Mind over matter*

                        Today the air is still
a raw sienna   settling ash —
            mist curls between conifers
in the ravine
the lake   all curves,   undulations

                  spanning the river
the bridge recedes,   languid,   arcing
invitation's quiet
utterance —

            All those unbridgeable
rifts across the years,   reaching for closure

Just kiss the rock
                  she said,   *move on*

while memories breach the levees —   tattered
                  whisper-thin

ii.   *The way light falls*

        reveals a darker side
to landscape's pastoral symmetry
behind the scenic veil

        A trail of severed
marigolds strewn across the field,   river's shrewd
        insistence —   rock's slivered
          face

        Yet today is summer
unmistakably —   only the kayak's silver silence
        a single breath of cloud
          piercing sky

        Our journey
worn by weight of moist air,   fabric's slight weft
                on skin —
light that falls   between image
        and knowing

Vectors

i.

Four sturdy pigeons   skirt
        the streetcar-tracks —   Richmond's Rock-
Doves   bluish-grey,   flying low —
they hold their ground,   strut and softly coo
           oblivious to the cruiser —   serving
and protecting,   its flashers red
as taxis   thread their way   between rails

ii.

       Slate-grey and pale
Peregrine Falcons   circle artificial cliffs
at Bay-and-Bloor —
narrow tails,   spots of black,   spectacular
                  on wing —
their long ascending wail,   their *kack-kack-kack*
and rasping   above
the brash   articulated crystals
          of the ROM

iii.

Shadow's burnt-sienna
shields ravines,   and corridors
of green —
Bohemian Waxwings'   grey-brown crests,   their
        rusty undertails,   and Mourning
Warblers —   elusive songbirds
        wintering-sleek

                each foraging beyond
the span   of *truss* and *arch*,   Parkway's sinuous
        reach,   wetlands of the Don

View from *The Miramar Hotel*

Bournemouth, Dorset

i.

Lime-green gardens
below my window,   an almost leafless tree
veined coral-dark
and then the sea
its ragged canvas   glazed viridian —
one small sailboat   angles into wind
a circling hawk,   and herring gulls' black wingtips
skirting waves —
in the distance,   barely visible,   the coastline —
Isle of Wight   to Purbeck Hills

ii.

        Tomorrow a scattering
of still-grey cloud   remembering
night's weight —
                pewter sea
    brushed-indigo,   wet-on-wet —   to the east
a splash of rose —   across the Channel
arcing skies,   the brashly-winding,   fearless
Grande Corniche —
all restless loops,   elegant geometries,   conjuring
      our wordless,   wine-dark swells

In Terms of Probabilities

i.

There are days
we seem to pivot separate earths —   our egg-shaped
perigees at odds with sun,   orbits
shifting like moons —
embraceably close,   more wishful convergence
than lunar nearness

Astronomers agree
we should gaze early and often   on Theia's lingerings
remnants from her fiery cloud,   moon's
dark / light coupling —
constant as the seas we see when
we lock eyes

ii.

It's time,   they say,   to put
the Now   back into physics —   our world a "heap of moments"
each   an instant's

woven memories
frozen-time

no escaping cul-de-sacs
trajectories re-shaped or thawed —   atoms   connected
light-years away —

even our clocks   can tick at
different rates —

their relative motion a kind of
strangeness

Density's dark energy
so fine-tuned —   with just the slightest shift,   life-giving-stars
would never have been formed

and we
would not be here

On Briefings: Notes and Other Anomalies

i.

       Weigh the question
where it leads,   ambiguity's plumb line
              falling Alice-like —
refresh filters,   hone
the lens —
for meaninglessness,   divide by zero
angles of rotation,   equal parts   of real —
then polish
       to solid shapes of loss

       Bear witness   where
you can   to absolutes —   twilight's reclusive
choreographies
a wood thrush,   its flute-songs
       and loon's sweet tremolo

ii.

       Search for subtlety
beyond the wall —   lower thresholds
entranceways
doorway's inside-edge,   penumbra's
       almost shadow

          attend to
counter-shading,   depth-of-field,   lest
you miss
a thin-curved start —   trace its path
      know its rules

     and breaking them
dream transformations,   mantle's
outer shell
      constantly re-shaped

Without Reserve

It's time to honour fissures
shards,   destruction
of clean lines —   take an axe to craft,   replace
          resin   with transparency

to be cradled   full-bodied
yet yielding —
soft curves at the lumbar side,   shams,   a quilted
                    bitter edge —
apple-whiff of smoke   dusted with herbs
          core   broken gold

II. Unmasked

Unmasked

On days   beyond
                    the reach of words
she conjures trees,   inner-root infusions
an elm,   palm,   an oak —
nodes and leaf-scars,   bark   applied to bole

all sacrament and crucible —
no sheathing base
no canopy   or crown,   layers exposed —

          field   from woodland
          stem from core —

canticles and incensations
bright grains   laid upon hot coals —

a fire's fragrant energy
summoning the smallest   sculpted word

Variations on a theme

        Take note of turbulence
the way a collar frames her face,   blouse
loosely falling —
                irruptions
of red admirals,   jewels on the wing

            claim all her lands
between high and low tide,   create ordinances
a chain-link fence
around heart's perimeter —
margins rough and rocked,   edges sharp in
        poem's lucent greening

Notturno

for *Great Jazz* by Wenda Watt
acrylic on canvas

A single shimmering utterance,   this saffron
                        gloss   of dreams —
            her name,   all willowish
            and wheaten —

The way she folds you in her gaze,   leans into orchids
                        after sunset —
            their sepals' yellow-green
                unfurling

Broken chords   darkening sweet —   a certain diffidence
                        her slender,   easy
        grace —   all auras and angels —
            a turquoise sweetness
                tinctured gold

On Process and Portrayal

The making of a portrait
of *The Honourable Mayann Francis,* by Mary Lou Payzant
acrylic on canvas

It's all in surrendering —   discernment,   stillness
brush-strokes' ineluctable web,   a painter's gaze —
allusive apprehensions   yielding face,   shadows
in the lower third,   values lightened —   ivory-black
and burnt-sienna   weaving hair —   touch of ochre-white
                    for muted greys

Likeness lives   in the way light falls on bone,   no replica
exact   even in a camera's shuttered eye —   shades
and dark   appearing deeper,   more punctuation than
detail —   this rendered glimpse into a subject's story
imprecise and gestural —   essences,   contour of a breast
                    the lower curve of lip

Colour,   straddling the crispest edge —   advancing
and receding yellow-warm,   crimson-cool —   introduce
conflicting hues   when darkening a skin-tone —   a mixed-in-
white maroon for warmth,   for subtlety,   burnt-umber —
                    all art *invention*   *in service*

Dreamscape: Intaglios

after *Black Ice: Prints by David Blackwood*

i.

       Luminous against the dark
your New Jerusalem —   a silhouette of peaks   hard-
edged,   tacking
into wind —   the sky   a steel-grey bruise

Ships at full-sail   flee the lash
tail and whale   breaching the rudderless deep —
those ghostly-cerulean
pinnacles and domes —   growlers'
        drifting rams   beneath the sea

ii.

       Easy to miss   that floundering
skiff,   barely-visible aquatint   wave-tossed
toward salvation
and the rock —   no sign of crew —   a time to invoke
last things,   acknowledge angels

angles,   closeness
of lines —   those intimate illusions   laboriously
incised,   mortality's dry brush
        your etchings'   blue-black ice

Point of Unravelling

after *Gossip* by G.A. Reid, R.C.A., 1888
oil on canvas

       Alone,   save
for the artist,   the spinning wheel
between them   still —
room's raw-umber,   hint of embers
solitary candle
clock's   upright blur —
       in window's light,   a tree

Perhaps it was the force of Newton's second law
that kept them there —

       her downward gaze
    intense and focused
    arm akimbo,   she leans into
    the wheel,   while you
    look upward —
    a ball of yarn coiled
    careless at your feet —
       the spindle   slack

a single axis
tautly-stretched —

        What words might frame
those tightly
buttoned dreams —
                apron's iceberg-blue
                                the jaunty tip of shoe
beneath your skirt,   folds soft-shadowing

How long   could such a gaze be held
'til more
            begins to unravel —

                who will risk
as angles shift —   yielding their dynamic
            ambiguities

Undertones

i.

Even a humpback whale
can turn tight circles,   move adeptly on the waves
          never lose its grip —

tapered,   geared to kill,   sharks
have no barnacles,   no comfortable fealties

no blue in feathers
of the Eastern Bluebird —   only wavelength's
          ambient light   bubbling
                    cerulean

ii.

All art an inch away —
elusive undertones,   too-tight-lavender eclipsing
          sage,   a skin's topography —

How an ocean sucks you in,   drift-and-return
its neutral buoyancy

truth's blurred décolletage —
          crests and hollows,   where light
                    bends

Even on such days

i.

arrival times matter for song birds —
what the wood thrush knows
as it tunes its flute-like whistle,   adjusts to weather
                    and to wind —
when a summer azure   folds its wings,   shelters
            in short grass

and petunias trail the flagstones,   shocking-pink on slate
hydrangea blooms
bending,   yet unbowed   above the stones,   ivy
                    thickly-silent
blanketing   the ageing cedar —   sun newly-crowned
            yet clearly now   dethroned

ii.

Even on such days,   amidst the flagstones and cedars
a volley of bullets   can shatter
            the city's centered calm —

victim and victimizer,   each a mother's child beneath
the swagger,   uniform
and gun —   matters of timing,   trajectory,   innocence
        lost,   voices stilled —
            all promise unfulfilled

What Luminous Veil

after *Don Valley on a Grey Day*, 1972, by William Kurelek
mixed media on hardboard

A winter city at its heart,   though not always
there *is* spring,   after all
                and kindness —
                        even your bridge,   benevolent
across a sweep of parkway,   footpaths,   trees
            sap-green silence

                On this grey day
the city glows,   asphalt tinged Precambrian-rose
            traffic flows —
no frantic sense of speed,   no helicopters overhead
            staccato reporters
                hovering

                Only the graceful,   curving Don
witness to a simpler past —   on the bridge,   a man and boy
            mindful father,   so unlike your own
                small girl   turning away,   gaze fixed
                        beyond the frame

No veils or chains blocking access   and the view —
            no modern Jeremiah here
                apocalypse,   after

Who among us   some-dark-day
hasn't considered a bridge
          measured weight of distance
                    torque of tractor-trailer

          the journey that brought you to this place
the Don contained,   river still —
          barely a hint
                    of cloud or shadow

          Beneath acrylic layers scrubbed clean —   morning's
                    hard grey grace

Ebb and Surge

We wake to double blue
　　　—May Swenson

Debussy　　held the sea's music in his blood —
　　　colours floating
　　　　　　　dawn to noon
percussive play of waves,　　muted horn —　　ocean's constant
　　　　mutability

a dialogue with wind　　vigorous,　　then languid
　　　all surge and ebb —
　　　　　　　　fortissimo,　piano
preludes we follow —　　water flowers,　　drowned cathedrals
　　　a garden　　steeped in rain

Slack tide, turning

for *Island at Low Tide* by Gail Read
oil on canvas

reveals the underside
probes moss and moon-snail,   their tender particularities
no sanctuary,   safe harbour
there —   just pine's shallow roots,   the sun and moon
radical   constancies

only at tide's ebb,   it's said,   will death appear

that longest possible
wave,   its disambiguation —   where you can track
hurts' turning   at slack tide
no walls of water,   flooding bore,   just inlets,   estuaries
coast's incision

depth measured
a point at a time,   soundings,   full disclosure —   as currents
move   and lines
fall out of true

Not even Ptolemy

This year's poems   refuse to hold —
they slip away
like raven feathers   cut for sound,   the harpsichord's
        quilled strings

perhaps it's the perils of confluence
gravity's lensing
light-beams' bend —   those unpredicted stars

They say not even Ptolemy
dared to care   whether his filigrees were real —

doubtless we'll need   enhanced economies of grace to
                account for what we see —
       enough   to hold a galaxy

III. Beyond Convergence

Because

                    words,   a mother's
tongue —   unleavened insinuations   wafer-thin,   desire's
            muffled womb

        because time
slips from its moorings,   because grief,   because prayer
                promise of a canvas
primed —   discernment's double-locked doors
            a tree's lost leaves

the advent of coincidence,   affirmation,   melting snow
        a crystal egg —
                because light comes
                            full circle

        because night
because there is no other —   just brush-strokes
            benediction,   an angel's
                    broken gravity

        where no tears fall

On Functions and Relations

Allow for symmetries
a conjecture of lines,   convergence
lightly-held —
waterstone,   verb's progress   tight-curled
          ephemera's

pigment,   voiles
and watermarks,   valley's veins,   arteries
stripped clean —
a single deep-lobed leaf,   nuance   feathering
                    cedars,   lark's

tongue   bevel-to-
edge —   pock-marked,   hammered
                    moonstone
vectored roots —   a calculus of curving
          assumptions   of true

Beyond Convergence

after *Lifelines & Lifelines 2*, images of photographic
art by Judith Davidson-Palmer

A poem echoes
in these roots and overlays —   their spidered
        paths,   pulse of veins
mapped green —
in manna-grass and willows
walnut-brown,   bank's indigo damp
        and sweet-gale traces   muted plum

It breathes ancient textured leaves
                        like vast lungs torn —
folds and fissures held   as river's dappled dark
reveals the poem's   chambered heart —
        its rib-like lines

        Angles of reflection
shifting —   random sightings   rhizomed-gold

Backwards Mapping

It seemed to be summer —
stubbled fields as far as one could see,   remnants of cut cane
fibres' contrary harvesting —
you push an empty cart with bamboo sides,   wooden wheels
anchored rims —
    seek enlightenment

Plot a path across
the highway,   a suddenly-cresting hill —   tractor-trailer to
your left   quickening —
hard to the right,   a solar wind,   coronal mass ejections
    uncertainty's   pivot

In breach
of un / broken lines —   released from the wheel,   crossing
    over   for good

No Solid Ground

       Night spins its vinyl
under strobes —
plays the same songs
familiar grooves and grievances
          over,   over

        shuffles through clutter —
layered folds of loneliness
carpeting floors —
lost prescriptions,   bills unpaid,   sealed
        sleeves of contact lenses

roams the universe
            of *what-ifs* and *should'ves*
for predictions and equations —

discrete differential geometries
in a violent splash of waves —   cable's
        shape
      how a needle   moves

Monkshood

Within its misting
shroud   the moon is brooding —
harbours cowled flowers,   autumn's last
                hypnotic bloom —
its dark-green foliage   and bulbous roots
       a poisoned cobalt-blue

Even on the darkest night,   we know the sky
will clear —
moon's clarity
             facet-sharp —
       not so   with scar formations in the stroma
cornea's clouding —
deepening blurs   of bronze and honey   elusive
      as neutrinos
            a searing opal haze

Coal Harbour Blues

You speak to me of absolutes,   your eyes
withholding nothing
Pain,   you say
                will do that —
strip away non-essentials,   stare truth
          and bad news down

Even books decline —   pages dog-eared
decay's reflection   cracked porcelain
          on a gilded vase

Along the seawall,   a demonstration —
voices chant
          above a sea of flags —
no one listens   across Burrard Inlet
not the unrelenting current —
its slate-grey flow
          indifferent as gulls
the harbour seals,   float planes landing
eddies and updrafts   peeling
               water's skin

Time to assume   an aerial stance,   weigh
probabilities —
               To be,   *or not*
          real questions,   in the end

Beyond the Red

       Perhaps a summer's ruby moon
strawberry-rose,   ochre-marbled sky,   the cubic
pull-and-push of planes —
       their meticulous   imperfections

Where lovers   shred & pluck
fierce harmonies —   glissandos balancing
       scabbard's edge

       A time for poems
groping their way through shadow,   cadence
by line   and covenant,   illusion's
       pigment

Like candles,   wine,   and red,   we know
these too   will wend their way
       and pass

Love's Conundrum

                    Impossible to miss
those mid-day cranes above the gridlock —
a city's steel-winged
choreography

          As lights turn green
          she eyes the jib,   recalls falling —
          love's pull
          of sheave and groove

the question —   *where do we fall*
as euphoria floods
the brain —
and ecstasy's alive   in fingertips

After the wildness
fall after-the-fall —   *what then*
attachment   as easy to drift   away
as into —

                    Best,   perhaps
to monitor planets,   reef sails before the storm
reduce the risk
of love's blind lingering —   its hoist and hook
                    its latticed boom

Slipstream

i.

Trusting travellers
we board our scheduled flights
light's ribboned thread   along each darkened aisle
caught
between substance and dream

mindful
of Anansi's nimble navigations
our rhymes unfurl —
their spinning webs
always at the ready —   arrows in time's
fleeting curve

ii.

                   Always practise lifeboat skills
when reversing
out of moorings,   watch for gulls and cormorants,   seaplanes
                           lunging swells

             Best to seize the slower advantage
in the slip —
cruiser's soft manoeuvre,   a mallard's cross-stitch,   lake-skin
                           giving sway

            Mindful of currents,   the four large carp
leaping from bondage
beneath the dock —   given enough time,   anything
                  that can happen   will

Of Gifts Too Rare

Perhaps it's true of love,   of beauty
both lie   in the gaze —

        one sole flame
        sufficing

        one lone candle
        you take

your chances —   pray
for reciprocation
a longer

        wick,   all gifts
        surrendered
        in the flowering
        deep shift

        then life —
        its random shuffling
        thud of cards,   play
        of the hand

no wisdom in the blindness
breath   or song
no honey
on the tongue

just   loss —
a double concerto's slow
         uncoupling
as note by note   slips shining by —

weeping pearls
a twisted lunar rope,   inevitable fading
         tapered grey

Sometimes

the most tender moments are hiding
in plain sight —
only clue a plaintive cry
               please find me
like our cat,   pleading for her mourning recognition

Maybe it's light wind,   brisk
on cusp of being
breeze —   some bite
          bracing enough,   but wanting —
wispy clouds,   cotton-furrowed,   springing azureous

still-naked trees   etched crystal-clear
astride the pavement —
a cedar fence
          its Payne's-grey canvas sunlit-
sliced —   in sidewalk's jagged cracks   a bold infusion

Like love   burned into grooves
impossible to lose —
still playing   well beyond —
                              invincible as web's
un-breachable tension,   its slender
          silk   fine-spun

IV. Fragments and Heartwood

In Mourning's Light

to name loss would be to lose it further
—Colm Tóibín

            Sunlight tracks along the ceiling
stitched into its white —
proclaims morning through shutters,   shadows precise as railway ties —
silent sculptured space,   clear as sunrise —
      a warbler's yellow-throated song
          mourning's edge

       space   she could
       slip into —
                        where gardens' ivied walls
           arch secular   yet cloistered
and ginger lilies press   grilles   oblivious to breath
or word —
all that could be
spoken —

wild banana's
green   exuberance
              heliconia,   pendulous
                 spiralling

one lone desert rose
      bent   in broken clay

Shifting to Low
on Gravity's Pull

i.

        Each day a journey
richly-veined,   rooting and up-rooting
to catch   light —
moon-phase,   contours and cartographies
        the pulse of bones

        even those certain palms
whose roots   are thick as arms,   rootless
Spanish Moss
where song birds nest,   whisk fern
        the tiniest duckweed

        conjuring their way
through bark and watershed —   following
gravity's pull
        in search of home

ii.

This summer Sunday
a woman considers   shifting
into low —
the two-lane regional road   newly-
paved   leads to The Valley of the Mother
                of God —

no angel sightings
            annunciations
                    flash of light
just incline's muscle —
irrevocable rush,   trees' faceless blur
                a verging-green momentum

beyond the crest
where shadows yawn and reach,   the un-
        mapped echo   of dunes

Independence:
Early Years

What is it about islands and anthems —
nostalgia's wistful yearning coiled   in back and limb
roots at home   routes away
                                    fascia's tightening
                        edginess of shores —

The summer we renewed our vows
Kingston dancehall-nights and moonlight   thrusting through
the convent's louvered windows —

    poverty,   chastity,   obedience,   service
      August's belching heat

       where the sun shines
No journey too far through Manchester's hills   for three young nuns
and their white Cortina station wagon,   fresh as Mandeville rain
and as persistent —
      soliciting for the high school fundraiser —
a farmer to donate the suckling for slaughter
the meat packer's freezer   where it hung for a week
a baker's midnight oven —
finished deed on spinning spits   that sparkling crowd-filled afternoon

      and the land is green

Not much older than her Fifth Form students
she mounts their poetry   on classroom walls —   reaches
                              for the syntax of freedom
                  home-turf semantics
                        pull of the sea

Those surprising moments,   shaded and imperfect,   when the sun
comes   conjuring truths —

                  curves and gestures   shoreline's limen
                        — grammars of authority —
                  the island's edges   everything

Fragments and Heartwood

i.

They say the roots of certain trees grow up,   not down
while some grow knees
                    interrupt the story —
                                plum,   baobab,   casuarina
        Bombay,   tamarind,   frangipani

                Anchors and deviations

                        Vendors with their baskets and wares
gathered each day   around the baobab —
girls tumbling from classrooms,   eager to spend their round bronze
pennies,   and tiny silver coins
        on grater cakes
                    gizzadas   and Bustamante's backbone

                        Mrs. Dalhouse,   with her large glass jar
of tamarind balls   twelve for sixpence
astute librarian,   year after year,   ignoring limits   for the girl
                    who lived   on a diet of books

                Some roots are permanent   and sweet

ii.

Today,   the air's like August in St. Andrew,   still and heavy
waiting for thunder —
        sharp, thick downpour flooding roads,   newly-minted potholes
            forcing traffic through and round —
                    each car   intent on seizing   its sliver
                        of advantage

                        Faced with obstacles,   roots thicken,   grow up
and over —
                sense gravity,   which way is down
                            perception at the tip

iii.

                                        Each life a galleria,   of sorts
self and world,   under constant
             observation —
                      stone,   resin,   leather,   wood

The boulder beneath bougainvillea   where she stood as a child
on July afternoons
carefully noting licence plates,   the provenance of cars
                          inching up Lady Musgrave Road —
the leisurely meander   of a herd of cows,   back from grazing
                 King's House grounds,
                      home of the British Governor

                          Some roots   are opportunistic
              others may need to be trimmed

iv.

Childhood certainties,   all sunlight and fierce truths —

Cable Hut,   its wild,   black-pebbled beach,   steep,   slack-drop
          to the sea,   waves' open mouth
and summers,   painting logos for her father's booth
at Denbigh Fair

               Pot a tree,   and roots will circle,   tie themselves
                              in knots

Time   a forest,   wood-breathing ribs,   polished smooth
          sapling,   mother to the tree

                              heartwood —
          limestone,   mountains
                    coral-sea

Lunar Eclipse

Partial to the sea,   he sailed the quays
          one eye on the heavens —
on clear nights   he would read the constellations
to his daughters —   sight Orion,   the Southern Cross

On the anniversary of his passing,   the moon turned
          blood orange —
stars in the milky way,   his winter solstice eclipse
                brilliantly aligned

As daylight hours slowly lengthen,   one daughter
          keeps close watch on weather
waits for efficacious winds,   perfect window for crossings

Attuned to signs and omens,   one writes
          reads the world —
newly-retired,   one recalibrates —   while another
                swallows silence

Tellers of tales,   they search for methods of reckoning —
          divining meanings
obscurities and secrets —   how to compute sea's equilibrium
          a hemisphere's surface —
when to surf a train of waves,   fetch wind's abandon
          take the measure of stars

Back View

for PJH

Remember a table
driftwood,   branch,   rock,   leaves —   squint
            see the shadows
                        says our art-teacher aunt
you tried your best,   saw nothing —
no slight insinuation
no still life

Today,   your house
sits snug   beyond an aging leafless oak —   its universe
        a pond   still as glass —
                        no need to squint,   close
your eyes —   you know what's there,   intimately —
each lived-in
corner,   turn of stair
cathedral ceiling,   span and sweep of windows —
        their darkest revelations
                and their light

Away

Beneath a dusking
pearl-grey-sky,   all seas   speak the same language —
a grammar's broken reef,   sands' glottal
keening

Night rides
ukulele-blues   above a restive surf —   later only *Kapalua*
whitecaps —   green eruptions,   craters
rising

As we summon
ice-floe clouds,   skirt turbulence and storms —   memory's
milky way   beyond our crescent moon's
waning

Notwithstanding Exclusions

Today,   the island's calm   between Pure Math
and Biology,   activity low at the Soufrière Hills Volcano —
two rockfalls,   one tectonic earthquake on the seismic network
                    Hazard Level: Two

last night in Old Towne   rain's ragged drum-beat silences cicadas
drenches tree frogs,   elusive galliwasps —
tomorrow,   when sunlight strokes the louvers,   the Salem Police
will inscribe her name
                    on a pass   to *Exclusion Zone C*

gutted remnants of volcanic molten fudge,   lunar landscapes
verging green —
stubborn fortitude of Yellow Warblers and bougainvillea
                    East at Jack Boy Hill

She could grow accustomed to pyroclastic flows
tracks across valleys frequently destroyed —   casual warnings
                    the exercise of caution —

mindful of wind's direction,   ground shifting —   ash-rain
mud-mix,   blackened-sky —
eruption's marrow in the bone,   the seismic pulse
                    ready   to outrun lava

Any waking morning

                              slipstream
or maelstrom —   need to brace,   step gingerly
retreat into page —
Five Go Adventuring,   A Girl of the Limberlost
The Rosary —   war-scarred worlds,   hot
            springs of Rotorua

                              tonguelash
castigations,   splintered air,   imprint of nails —
time to consult
her grandfather's   *Encyclopaedia Britannica*
ponder   consequential geographies
            the *arrangement*
of unequal things —   passion,   power —   *Tyger*
            Tyger,   graceful tildes —   *canta*
                  y no llores

On the Way to Andalusia

                    I am searching
for my mother —
                              sense her in
the dance,   its calculated frenzy carefully rehearsed
heels,   hands
                    body's torque —
in poem's slant insinuations,   all fears forgone
forgiven —   where language burns
          its deep songs   weeping

Fall into Freedom

       She roams the garden
in dream —   bypasses Adam,   venom
of snakes,   no stone unturned —
attends to coincidence,   whirlpools,   conflux —
       crucifix and sacrifice

       encounters Eve,   skin on skin
bronzed and confident —   *honey and milk   under*
her tongue
conjures river and sea,   rock against wave,   tells it —
       winter past
                  rains over and gone

On Distillations

No need to engage   colloidal silver's
                    nano-particles
she's been given the all-clear for stress,   anxiety
anger —   no firm
sense though,   how she's doing with love and joy —
by all accounts
and anecdotal evidence
            things seem   promising

perhaps,   it's the placebo effect,   flax fibre
or inner bark of mulberry —
felt and felt-sense
                    life's yellows and azure blues
                            lurching green

arias that stir
still-tender wounds —   melodic overlays
their descant echoes
                veiled —   all silvered memories
                        annulled

Deep-Water Benediction

i.

Finally,   no coral breath,   or sand,   no sun
just water's marbled urgency,   a body's longing —   still
deep enough   for drowning

Alternate days   she seeks out words,   gathers them
close beneath her ribs
                                        slips into page
                            adrift   in memory's wash —
Sundays at the Rockforth springs,   Flat Bridge spanning
            Rio Cobre's gorge,   the Martha Brae

ii.

Each night,   mercy's prayer —
absolution's ashes,   salt,   and wine

those crystal-cloud insinuations,   blue holes,   pools
and waterfalls —
                    where a river   goes to ground

From the doorway,   both rooms
the cats curled into dreams,   crimson pillows' silent
waiting —
            water's lustrous language   like skin

Notes

I: The Way Light Falls

"In Matters of Art"
This poem was influenced by information on Higgs boson, the elusive God Particle, and Tonia Cowan's graphic article "The God Particle: The Heart of the Matter" in *The Globe and Mail*, Thursday, July 5, 2012.

"Musings on the Lakeshore Line"
The poem had its beginnings on the GO Train Lakeshore line between Toronto and Oakville, Ontario.

"Vectors"
See *Birds of Toronto: A Guide to Their Remarkable World* (City of Toronto Biodiversity Series, City of Toronto, 2011); *The Audubon Society Field Guide to North American Birds, Eastern Region*, by John Bull and John Farrand Jr., Visual Key by Susan Rayfield (A Chanticleer Press Edition). The Bloor Viaduct is a *truss and arch* bridge, one of several bridges in Toronto that span the Don River and the Don Valley Parkway.

"Views from The Miramar Hotel"
I stayed at the Miramar Hotel in Bournemouth, England, in October 2011. The hotel was a favourite haunt of J. R. R. Tolkien and it's widely accepted that he did much of his writing there.

"In Terms of Probabilities"
A variation on a found poem, gleaned primarily from the following sources:

i) "Discoveries Point to a Violent Birth for the Moon," by Natalie Angier, Science & Technology, *New York Times International Weekly*, Weekend, September 20, 2014. In Greek mythology, Theia was the mother of Selene, goddess of the moon.

ii) "Resetting the Clocks," by Alan Lightman, a review of *Time Reborn: From the Crisis in Physics to the Future of the Universe* by theoretical physicist Lee Smolin (Houghton Mifflin Harcourt, 2013), *The New York Times Book Review*, Sunday, May 5, 2013.

The phrase "heap of moments" is a quote from British physicist and philosopher Julian Barbour cited in the Lightman review.

"On Briefings: Notes and Other Anomalies"
Section ii was influenced by the op-ed "At the Edge of Inside" by David Brooks, *The New York Times Opinion Pages*, June 24, 2016; information on "edge detection" and "the formation of shells" (see Wikipedia.org).

"Without Reserve"
This poem began as a variation on a found poem triggered by "Beautiful because it's broken" by Signe Langford, Globe Life & Arts/Furniture, *The Globe and Mail*, Thursday, March 12, 2015, and by "Tuscany for the Win" by Beppi Crosariol, Globe Style/Wine & Spirits, *The Globe and Mail*, Saturday, March 7.

II: Unmasked

"Unmasked"
A version of this poem was written for *Night of the Elm* by Gail Read, watercolour on paper, 23 ½ x 19 ¼ inches.

"On Process and Portrayal"
The Honourable Mayann Francis, Lieutenant Governor of Nova

Scotia from 2006 to 2012, was the first African Nova Scotian appointed to the position. The phrase in italics is from a quote attributed to Petrarch: "If true facts are lacking, add imaginary ones. Invention in the service of truth is not lying."

"Dreamscape: Intaglios"
Inspired by the Art Gallery of Ontario exhibition *Black Ice: Prints by David Blackwood*, in particular *Haven,* 1994, etching and aquatint on paper; and *Weseleville Fleet in Labrador Sea,* 1995, etching and aquatint on paper. Blackwood is known for his intaglio prints — the opposite of relief printing — done from ink that's below the surface of the plate. The design is cut, scratched, or etched into the printing surface, or plate. "Growlers" are icebergs less than 6' 6" that float with less than 3' 3" showing above the water.

"Point of Unravelling"
A play on Newton's second law in relation to net forces acting in opposite directions in a spinning wheel: "A net force F1 must act on particles in the top half of the wheel and a net force F2 must act on particles in the bottom half of the wheel." The painting *Gossip* by G. A. Reid was on exhibition in the Art Gallery of Ontario.

"Undertones"
The phrase "all art   an inch away" is a riff on the words of Geoffrey Dyer that "most of his writing is 'only an inch away from life — but all the art is in that inch.' " Referenced in Clancy Martin's review of Dyer's work entitled "The Wordy Shipmate." The image "how/ an ocean sucks you in" suggested by the description of "A 'neutral buoyancy' ... " a point about 30 feet below the surface that freedivers know as 'neutral buoyancy.' Beneath it, the ocean stops trying to spit you out and begins sucking you in."

"Ebb and Surge"
Suggested by titles and musical images in Debussy's *La Mer* (The

Sea), *Jardins sous la pluie* (Gardens in the Rain), *Fleur des eaux* (Water flower) and *La Cathédrale engloutie* (The Sunken Cathedral). The epigraph is from May Swenson's "Early Morning: Cape Cod," *The Complete Love Poems of May Swenson*, Foreword by Maxine Kumin (Houghton Mifflin, Boston, 2003) p. 4.

"Slack tide, turning"
Italicized lines, *"only at tide's ebb, it's said, will death appear,"* suggested by the following: "the belief that people at the coast will only die as the tide goes out … has been around for a long time, as shown by Thomas Tusser's *Five Hundred Points of Good Husbandrie* (1557): 'Tyde flowing is feared for many a thing / Great danger to such as be sick it doth bring' (xiv, stanza 4); it is also mentioned by Pliny (*Natural History* [A.D. 77], i. 128) quoting Aristotle. English references continue well into the second half of the twentieth century."

"Not even Ptolemy"
Variations on a found poem informed by the following:

i) "Quills from raven feathers are cut so that they create a uniform sound when used to pluck the strings inside a harpsichord" from "The Science of Bach" by Trish Crawford, *Toronto Star,* Sunday, May 3, 2015.

ii) An example of a theory that "can account for what we see without necessarily describing reality" is the "geocentric model of the heavens that Ptolemy laid out … with the planets orbiting the Earth along paths of complex curlicues …. Ptolemy apparently didn't care whether his filigrees were real." Source: "The Perils Associated with Dark Matter" by George Johnson, *Toronto Star – The New York Times International Weekly*, Weekend May 2–3, 2015.

iii) The phrase "enhanced economies / of grace" was suggested by the title of the Khinder Wyle art exhibition, *The Economy of Grace,* the Sean Kelly Gallery, New York, 2015.

III: Beyond Convergence

"On Functions and Relations"
The poem was the inspiration for *Lifelines and Lifelines 2* by Judith Davidson-Palmer, Fine Art Photography on Archival Paper, Limited Editions, each 3 of 10, 17" x 22".

"Beyond Convergence"
"Beyond Convergence" was written for *Lifelines & Lifelines 2,* images of photographic art created by Judith Davidson-Palmer in response to my poem "On Functions and Relations." The "ancient textured leaves" in Judith's photograph are from the Giant Gunnera plant. It evolved 150 million years ago around the time of the dinosaurs and can have a leaf span of seven feet. The photograph was taken in Royal Horticultural Society (RHS) Harlow Carr Garden, Harrogate, North Yorkshire. The river/wetlands in the second photograph is the Trent River in Peterborough, Ontario.

"No Solid Ground"
"The field of 'discrete differential geometry' involves ... precise mathematical equations based on the way the world looks and operates." Source: "Serious Math That Perfects Animation" by Patricia Cohen, *The New York Times, Sunday Star,* Sunday, January 23, 2011.

"Monkshood"
Suggested by *The Globe and Mail* article "*Aconitum fisheri* 'Monkshood'" by Marjorie Harris, Globe Style, Saturday, Oct. 24, 2015. The "stroma" is the thickest layer of the cornea and maintains its transparency. "Corneal abrasions usually heal rapidly ... however, deep corneal involvement may result in... scar formation in the stroma."

See article "Corneal Abrasion" (Author: Arun Verma, MD; Chief Editor: Hampton Roy Sr., MD).

"Love's Conundrum"
Influenced in part by excerpts from the article "Where Do We Fall When We Fall in Love?" by philosopher and psychoanalyst Elizabeth Young-Bruehl, published in the *Journal for the Psychoanalysis of Culture and Society* 8.2 (2003) 279–288. A sheave is a wheel with a groove for a rope to run on.

"Of Gifts Too Rare"
Both title and poem are a riff on the lines "*a gift too rare / will in surrender fade*" from May Swenson's poem "Say You Love" from *The Complete Love Poems of May Swenson*; Foreword by Maxine Kumin (Houghton Mifflin, Boston, 2003) p. 143.

IV: Fragments and Heartwood

"In Mourning's Light"
The epigraph is an abbreviated quote from Colm Tóibín's insightful essay *On Elizabeth Bishop* (Princeton University Press, Princeton and Oxford, 2015) p. 126. The full quote is "… to name the loss would be to lose it further."

"Shifting to Low/ on Gravity's Pull"
On Airport Road, an Ontario highway between Toronto and Stayner, there's a sign that lets drivers know they are approaching The Valley of the Mother of God.

"Independence:/ Early Years"
The lines "*where the land is green; and the sun shines*" are variations on the explanation of two of the three colours of the Jamaican flag — green and gold, respectively. "*poverty,   chastity,   obedience, service*" are words from the vows taken by members of the Order

of Religious Sisters of Mercy. Found images "roots at home/ routes away," and "edginess" are from "Littoral Space(s): Liquid Edges of Poetic Possibility" by Suzanne Thomas, *Journal of the Canadian Association for Curriculum Studies*, Spring/Summer 2007.

"Fragments and Heartwood"
After Guiseppe Penone's tree-sculpture, *Cedro di Versailles*, installed for several years in the Galleria Italia of the Art Gallery of Ontario. Grater cakes, gizzadas and Bustamante's backbone are Jamaican coconut candies. Bustamante's backbone is named after Sir Alexander Bustamante, one of Jamaica's National Heroes and the island's first Prime Minister. It is said to represent his firmness of character. Lines on roots informed by various sources on plant biology cited on the web.

"Lunar Eclipse"
The nineteenth anniversary of my father's death coincided with the rare lunar eclipse of December 21, 2010, "the first one to fall on the winter solstice in more than 300 years, according to NASA … (The) president of the Royal Astronomical Society of Canada said this eclipse will be particularly beautiful because it is one of the rare times the moon will be aligned with stars of the Milky Way … Hindu scripture says an eclipse is an attempt by the demon Rahu to swallow the moon." Source: "Skygazing: Anticipating a rare lunar eclipse; Swallowed moon, coinciding with winter solstice, may reveal shades of orange and brick red." *The Globe and Mail*, Monday, December 20, 2010.

"Back View"
PJH refers to my sister, Pamela Joan Hall.

"Notwithstanding Exclusions"
After a reading/presentation at the 2013 Montserrat Alliouaguana Festival of the Word. *Alliouaguana* is the Kalinago-Taino (Carib-

Arawak) name for the island of Montserrat and the name by which the yearly festival is known.

"Any waking morning"
Book and poetry references: *The Five Go Adventuring Again* by Enid Blyton (1943); *A Girl of the Limberlost* by Gene Stratton-Porter (1909); *The Rosary* by Florence L. Barclay (1909); "Tyger Tyger" from William Blake's poem "The Tyger," *Songs of Innocence and Experience* (1789). The italicized quote "...*arrangement of unequal things...*" is from *Canada* by Richard Ford referenced in "Points North," review by Andre Dubus III, *The New York Times Book Review,* Saturday, June 10, 2012. The Spanish "*canta y no llores*" (loosely translated: "sing, don't cry") is from "Cielito Lindo," a Mexican ranchera song.

"Fall into freedom"
The line "honey and milk   under her tongue" is a variation on verse 11, Song 4, The Bridegroom, *The Song of Songs.* The lines "winter past/   rains over and gone" are a variation on verse 11, Song 2, The Bride, The Song of Songs. An earlier version was influenced by the painting *Kind of Blue* by Wendy Weaver, acrylic on paper, 32" x 24."

"On Distillations"
Colloidal silver consists of silver atoms suspended in distilled ion-less water. The particles of silver are small enough to penetrate on a cellular level and destroy pathogens of all types. Thanks to Janet Neilson, RN, MSc HD, for an introduction to colloidal silver.

"Deep-Water Benediction"
Rockforth baths is a mineral spa along Kingston harbour in Jamaica. "The water rises from cold mineral springs in the hills above, and flows through the bath and into the sea under the main road." Source: Olive Senior, *Encyclopedia of Jamaican Heritage* (2003), Twin Guinep Publishers, St. Andrew, Jamaica, pp. 423–424. Built by the Spaniards, the flat bridge is one of Jamaica's oldest bridges. It

crosses the Rio Cobre (Spanish for "Copper River"). The Martha Brae is another of Jamaica's rivers.

Publication Credits

"Musings on the Lakeshore Line," "Variations on a theme" and "Because" — Earlier versions in "Women Writing 4: Remembering," *Canadian Woman Studies Journal/les cahiers de la femme* (Winter 2012/ Spring 2013).

"No Solid Ground" — Earlier version in *Quills, Canadian Poetry Magazine.*

"Independence:/ Early Years" — Earlier version in *Jubilation! Poems Celebrating 50 Years of Jamaican Independence*, edited by Kwame Dawes (Leeds: Peepal Tree Press, 2012).

"Fragments and Heartwood" — Published in the chapter: "Where Surf Meets Shore: Reflections from the Edge" in *Jamaica in the Canadian Experience: A Multiculturalizing Presence,* edited by Carl E. James and Andrea Davis (Eds.) (Halifax & Winnipeg: Fernwood Publishing, 2012).

"Fall into Freedom" — Earlier version published in the chapter: "Joys and Dilemmas, Documenting, Disentangling, and Understanding Experience through Poetry" in *Poetic Inquiry II — Seeing, Caring, Understanding, Using Poetry as and for Inquiry*, edited by Kate T. Galvin and Monica Prendergast (Rotterdam: Sense Publishers, 2016).

Acknowledgements

My gratitude to Luciana Ricciutelli, Editor-in-Chief, Inanna Publications, for continuing to believe in my work and for all that goes into producing a beautiful book.

Thanks to artist Judith-Davidson Palmer for the evocative painting that graces the cover, to Allan Briesmaster for his thoughtful editorial comments; and to Jean L. Stinson for her meticulous proof-reading / formatting and friendship.

My appreciation to the poets of the Long Dash group, Elana Wolff, John Oughton, Merle Nudelman, Sheila Stewart, Clara Blackwood, Kath Maclean and Yaqoob Gaznavi (deceased) for ongoing friendship and insightful feedback.

The trajectory of several poems were influenced/inspired by the work of artists Gail Read, Wenda Watt, Judith Davidson-Palmer, Mary Lou Payzant, Wendy Weaver and Marjorie Moeser. All were Studio Artist members of the Women's Art Association of Canada and participants in a long running ekphrastic collaboration with poets from the Long Dash group. Thanks also to Sue Macleod for her poetry workshop at the Art Gallery of Ontario which led to poems influenced by the work of David Blackwood, G.A. Reid, William Kurelek and Guiseppe Penone.

And to my partner, Anne-Marie Caron-Reaume, my enduring thanks for her caring presence.

Mary Lou Soutar-Hynes is a Jamaican-Canadian, poet/educator and former nun. A Fellow at Scotland's Hawthornden International Retreat for Writers in Fall, 2009, her literary publications include the collections: *Dark Water Songs* (2013); *Travelling Light* (2006), long-listed for the 2007 ReLit Poetry Award; and *The Fires of Naming* (2001). Published in Canada, the UK, and The Netherlands, her work includes poetry and essays in journals and anthologies and chapters in edited books. She lives in Toronto.